Remote Mob Programming

At home, but not alone.

Jochen Christ
Simon Harrer
Martin Huber

Foreword by Mark Pearl

ISBN 978-3-9821126-0-2
innoQ Deutschland GmbH
Krischerstraße 100 · 40789 Monheim am Rhein · Germany
Phone +49 2173 33660 · WWW.INNOQ.COM

Layout: Tammo van Lessen with X͇ƎL͏ATͤX
Design: Sonja Scheungrab
Print: Pinsker Druck und Medien GmbH, Mainburg, Germany

Remote Mob Programming
Published by innoQ Deutschland GmbH
1st Edition · August 2019

Contents

Foreword

When I was first introduced to Mob Programming, it was as something we did together in person.

Because of the benefits I had seen from mobbing I decided to write a book on it.

One of the first questions my editor had for me was could this be done remotely?

My own team had experimented with mobbing remotely with limited success and I was doubtful if remote work and mob programming could ever work effectively together.

I'm happy to see that Simon, Jochen and Martin have proven me wrong.

They are the first team I've come across to document how to mob effectively for long periods of time while working remotely.

I'm very pleased to see them share their insights with the rest of the world.

Turns out it is possible to have the convenience of remote work and the power of mob programming at the same time.

This is a must read for anyone wanting to do both.

Mark Pearl
Author of Code with the Wisdom of the Crowd[1]

---

[1] https://pragprog.com/book/mpmob

Remote Mob Programming

Remote Mob Programming combines two ways of working: Mob Programming and working as a distributed team. Woody Zuill describes Mob Programming[1] as creating the "same thing, at the same time, in the same space, and on the same computer". Working in the same space clashes with working as a distributed team at first glance, but actually, it goes together really well. With Remote Mob Programming, a team collaborates closely in the same virtual space.

We're working as software engineers at INNOQ. In our projects, we experienced very different ways of developing software, both on-site and remote. And at INNOQ, we always challenge the status quo, trying to find better ways to collaborate.

In August 2018, three of us started a project together. For the project kick-off, we came together on-site for two weeks. We quickly decided that we wanted to develop the first components together to discuss architecture and find a common code style. For that, we used Mob Programming on-site. This worked out pretty well, so we wanted to continue working so intensely together from our home offices. So we simply tried out Mob Programming remotely.

We even came to realize that Remote Mob Programming is superior to anything we ever tried before.

We do Remote Mob Programming full-time every day for over a year now. One year without daily stand-ups. One year without waiting for code reviews. One year without handovers before holidays. One year

---

[1] https://mobprogramming.org

at home without feeling alone. We don't want to work differently anymore.

We've written up our experiences. And we'd like to encourage you to try it out as well! Happy reading!

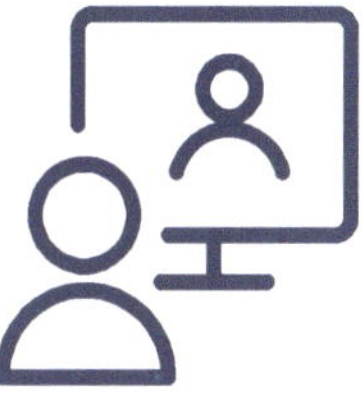

Remote Everybody

To collaborate well in a distributed team, it is essential that everybody works remotely by default. It does not work if part of the team shares a room. This would lead to information asymmetry[2] through communication shortcuts. That typically happens in on-site meetings with a few remote attendees.

The issue with working from home is isolation. It lacks the exchange with colleagues in the hallway, during lunch, or after meetings.

We all work from home, but don't feel alone.

We enjoy working from home: a quiet environment, perfect working setup, no commuting, and more quality time with our families and friends. With Remote Mob Programming, we constantly communicate with everybody in our team. It feels like being in the same room. And it is real team work.

---

[2]https://en.wikipedia.org/wiki/Information_asymmetry

Camera Always On

Working face-to-face is powerful because we communicate with the whole body, not just our words. Rolling eyes, yawning, looking pensive, or raising an eyebrow are just a few examples for that.

We activate our cameras all the time.

It felt strange at first, but after a few days, it became natural. It gives a sense of presence in the team, almost like working in the same room together. It helps to see if someone is away from keyboard, talking to their children, or otherwise distracted.

In a multi-monitor setup, we make sure that the camera is at our main screen so that you're looking at each other. We mute our microphones when we go away from the keyboard, but leave the camera on.

Regular On-Site Meetings

The better everybody knows each other, the better everybody can collaborate remotely. Getting to know each other still works best on-site. Drinking cold beverages together online with a virtual fireplace running on the shared screen just isn't the same.

We work together on-site once a month.

In the last few months, we met in awesome cities with good transport links, had barbecue at someone's home, or came together at one of the INNOQ events[3]. Some tasks are more effective face-to-face. That's why we prefer to hold retrospectives, discuss strategy, and think through the next epic on these days. And have fun together in real life.

---

[3] https://www.innoq.com/blog/st/2012/09/innoq-company-events

Same Time

One of the prerequisites of Mob Programming is working at the same time.

We mob six hours a day.

We align our core working hours, giving up some flexibility of typical remote work. We also agree on the same lunch hour. Still, it's totally OK to have an external meeting, get your hair cut, or spend time with the family. Mob Programming can be quite exhausting, so make room for breaks.

Typist and the Rest of the Mob

We prefer the terminology from Code with the Wisdom of the Crowd by Mark Pearl[4]:

One person controls the keyboard, this is the *typist*. The *rest of the mob* discusses the problem, agrees on the solution, and instructs the typist. The typist follows their instructions, puts them into code, and may ask clarifying questions to understand the solution. The rest of the mob guides the typist as needed.

We value the typist as they allow the rest of the mob to focus on solving the problem.

The typist must not code on their own. This balances the participation of all team members and it reduces the dominance of strong characters.

---

[4] https://pragprog.com/book/mpmob

Screen Sharing

The typist shares their primary screen, showing the code, ticket, or wiki the team is working on. It is highly efficient to work with the actual artifact in contrast to having abstract meta discussions.

We all look at the same shared screen.

Looking at and working on the same issue forces us to focus. It is good practice to use fullscreen and disable notifications.

We accept the time penalty to switch the shared screen at the start of the next mob interval.

We tried collaboration IDEs. Surprisingly, this lead to worse collaboration. Impatient members just hacked in their ideas, circumventing the mob. With screen sharing, the rest of the mob must explain what to do through language. No shortcuts.

10 Minute Intervals

Every mob session has a specific goal (e.g. to implement a feature or fix a bug) and may last several hours. In a mob session, the typist role rotates periodically. Short rotation periods keep everyone concentrated and every opinion in the mix.

We rotate every ten minutes.

We tried different rotation periods and considered ten minutes as a good trade-off. Shorter periods didn't work out for us because of the inherent switching costs in a remote team.

Surprisingly, taking your turn as a typist allows you a mental relaxation. You just wait for instructions.

Git Handover

With on-site Mob Programming, you just pass on the keyboard to hand over to the next person. This is a challenge for a distributed team.

We hand over with WIP commits on a temporary git branch.

To have a clean master branch, we work on a temporary *mob-session* branch. After each interval, we push a work in progress (WIP) commit to this branch. In this branch, we don't care about the commit message, if the code compiles, or if the tests are green.

A quick handover is essential. At the end of the mob session, we squash[5] the WIP commits into expressive commits and merge into master.

We created a small command line tool mob[6] to simplify the handover through git.

<hr>

[5] https://git-scm.com/book/en/v2/Git-Tools-Rewriting-History
[6] https://github.com/remotemobprogramming/mob

Small Team

The whole team works and focuses on the same thing. Only one person can talk at the same time. With larger teams, the individual speaking time shrinks, making it harder to stay focused. It is easy to become mentally absent. Also, expect technical issues, such as connectivity problems or interfering noise, to happen more frequently in a larger team. Those issues will block the whole team.

We have a team of four.

Obviously, the minimum size to form a mob is three. In our experience, teams with three to four developers provide the best benefit-cost ratio. A team of four has the great benefit of still being able to form a mob, even if one person is absent.

Regardless of your team size, make sure that every member takes on the typist role every 30 to 45 minutes to stay focused. Our team of four works well with a 10-minute rotation.

Group Decisions

In software engineering, you constantly compare different alternatives and decide for one. Reversing decisions is often expensive. Group decisions are superior over individual decisions[7]. In Remote Mob Programming, all decisions are group decisions.

We minimize technical debt.

With our wealth of know-how, experience, and opinions to discuss, we are able to make well-founded decisions everyone agrees with. When we are coding, we all agree on changes and code style. As a consequence, we don't need code reviews or pull requests.

We document decisions with extensive consequences using Architecture Decision Records[8].

---

[7] https://environmentalevidencejournal.biomedcentral.com/articles/10.1186/s13750-016-0066-7

[8] http://thinkrelevance.com/blog/2011/11/15/documenting-architecture-decisions

Constant Momentum

In a feature branch-based workflow, you are blocked waiting for the code review of your pull request. While waiting, you start another feature and need to switch context. In a mob session, we have continuous and implicit code reviews – no feature branches, no waiting, no context switches.

Working alone, you often end up looking up things on Google, in a documentation, or need to figure out how to proceed. The main purpose of the rest of the mob is to make sure there is constant momentum. They discuss the problem and think ahead towards the solution, getting rid of any obstacles.

We frequently get into a rewarding flow.

As we aren't blocked by ourselves, we make good progress. It feels great.

Learn from the Team

Sharing knowledge is at the heart of Mob Programming.

Everything the mob does is the result of in-depth discussions. Nothing is done without agreeing on the why. That's where everybody learns.

We get better by learning from each other.

Because the whole teams works on everything together, we're always on the same level of knowledge and have a bus factor[9] of the size of the team. We benefit from our different backgrounds and perspectives. This ranges from learning how to write a good unit test, to debugging effectively, or learning how to prepare a successful meeting. And we also learn a lot of keyboard shortcuts all the time.

With Mob Programming, onboarding only takes weeks, not years.

---

[9] https://en.wikipedia.org/wiki/Bus_factor

Trust

We all work remotely. The client does not *see* us working. So, management has a natural fear of losing control over the team.

Also, there is inherent doubt of a team's productivity, with all team members working on the same issue at the same time.

We build trust by communicating actively.

While management showed us some trust in advance, eventually we earned it through continuous and sincere communication and always delivering what we committed to.

We write daily check-ins[10] in our team's chat channel. A check-in is a short recap of stuff that happened or hasn't worked out as planned. It could be some personal stuff, too. Management also reads this channel and thereby is informed. Obviously, we have no need for a Daily Scrum[11].

We always take care to hold to our commitments and deliver high quality code in time. That builds solid trust in the long term.

---

[10] https://basecamp.com/features/checkins
[11] https://www.scrum.org/resources/what-is-a-daily-scrum

Save the Planet

Daily commuting causes traffic jams, crowded trains, and significant greenhouse gas emissions. Even worse, many consultants fly to their customers' offices.

We don't travel, so zero emissions.

No travel means no travel costs for us and our customers. And at home, we always drink our fair-traded flat white from our Star Wars mugs.

Dine with your Family

As software engineers, we often struggle to balance challenging and rewarding work with time for family and leisure. Sometimes, it feels mutually exclusive. From our experience, working on challenging and rewarding projects as a part of an outstanding team requires lots of travelling, staying in hotels overnight, and sometimes even relocation.

We enjoy more quality time with our families.

We all have young kids. They are the most important thing in our lives. With Remote Mob Programming we get both, rewarding work and quality time with our families and kids.

Our Setup

A variety of software and hardware make our way of working possible.
We evaluated a range of services and devices, and even created a small
software tool by ourselves. In this section, we describe the tools we
ended up with to mob together remotely every day.

Video Conferencing

We use video conferencing and screensharing all day long. That's why
the tools must be reliable and usable.

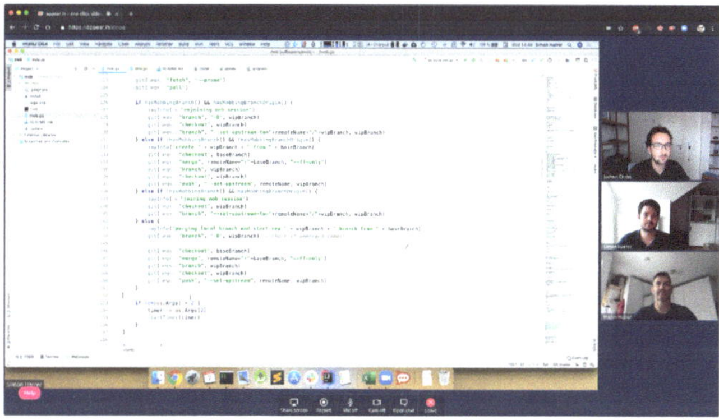

Remote Mob Programming with Whereby

We started using *Whereby*. The concept of virtual rooms as URLs, not
bound to a single person, has been and still is a perfect fit for Remote
Mob Programming. At the start of the day, the room simply fills up

until the mob can start after a little bit of small talk. Technology-wise, Whereby uses WebRTC within the browser supporting up to 12 people. This allows anybody to easily join the virtual room without installing any software, simply by entering the URL of the virtual room in the browser. Life was great until a Linux-developer joined our team. WebRTC requires so much processing power on Linux that it slows down everything else. That's why we had to have a look around for alternatives.

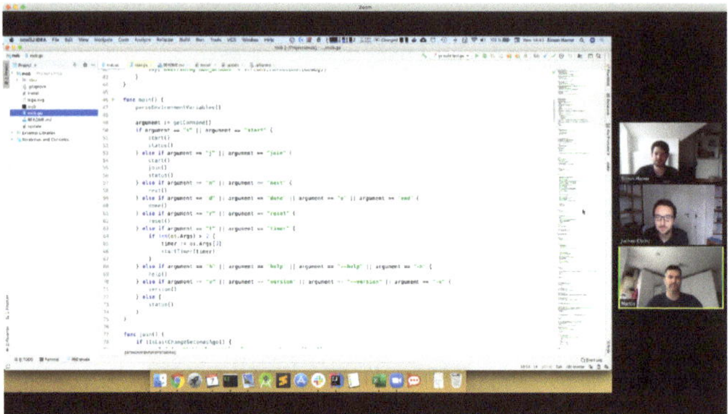

Remote Mob Programming with Zoom

We ended up using *Zoom*. Simply because it works well on Linux as its native client requires less CPU. Plus you can have up to 100 people in your session, although you probably don't want to. So, in summary, Zoom works for us, but it has its limitation as well. It lacks the concept of virtual rooms so you need a host for every meeting. And because it requires the installation of a native client, it's a little bit of a hassle to get people in our session for a quick help.

Microphone

Great audio is essential. Background noise or echos all day long is really exhausting.

That's why we all bought a studio microphone, the *Blue Yeti Microphone*. This microphone felt like a liberation, because we no longer had to wear headsets all day long, every day of the week. It works great in our quiet home office environment. And it even generates a feel of sitting right next to each other.

Blue Yeti Microphone

Make sure that you configure it right. Set the input pattern to cardioid mode, optimized for voices directly in front of the microphone. But be aware that the microphone is very sensitive – it will transmit even smaller noises quite clearly, such as eating crisps.

Camera

We feel most comfortable having the camera on eye level. But that's really hard with laptop cameras, as they often result in a frog perspective. And in our home office, we enjoy working on our large external screens. We recommend the *Logitech C920 HD Pro Webcam* as it can be mounted on top of external screens.

Logitech C920 HD Pro Webcam

Whiteboard

Quickly sketching out an idea is important. We missed the whiteboard in our remote setting and looked for solutions. We haven't found a perfect replacement yet. The best alternative we did find, however, is using an *iPad* with an *Apple Pencil* in combination with a collaborative whiteboard such as *Miro*.

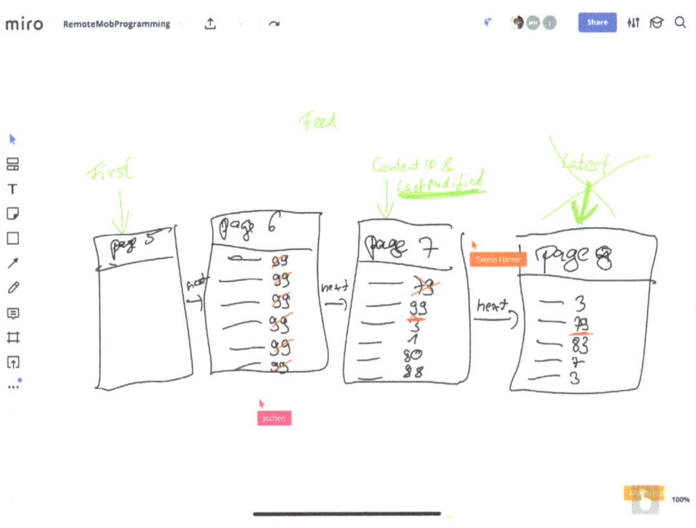

Collaborative Whiteboard with Miro

Handover

A quick handover keeps the flow. We developed a small tool called *mob* that simplifies a handover through git. It pushes any changes to a temporary branch from which the next typist pulls. And it starts a timer. It's written in Go and freely available on GitHub[1].

```
→ fizzbuzz git:(master) mob start 10
 ✓ [git fetch --prune]
 ✓ [git pull]
 > create mob-session from master
 ✓ [git checkout master]
 ✓ [git merge origin/master --ff-only]
 ✓ [git branch mob-session]
 ✓ [git checkout mob-session]
 ✓ [git push --set-upstream origin mob-session]
 ✓ 10 minutes timer started (finishes at approx. 18:41)
 > mobbing in progress

→ fizzbuzz git:(mob-session) mob next
 ✓ [git add --all]
 ✓ [git commit --message "Mob Session DONE [ci-skip]"]
 ✓ [git push origin mob-session]
README.md | 2 ++
 1 file changed, 2 insertions(+)
 ✓ [git checkout master]
```

Typical Usage of the mob *tool*

---

[1] https://github.com/remotemobprogramming/mob

FAQ

How to convince my boss?

Don't ask. Just try it out. And then share your experiences with your boss.

How to convince my boss if they really ask?

Time to market is optimized. That's because with the combined knowledge of the team, the team can immediately solve problems and make well-founded decisions – that's the power of Mob Programming.

And with Remote Mob Programming, you get access to a large pool of remote developers who spend less on travel. But in the end, we assume it's time to market that makes the difference.

Is Remote Mob Programming something for every team?

Remote Mob Programming is intense collaboration. This can be great, or it will quickly reveal any team dysfunctions. We think it's definitely worth a try.

Isn't one of the main benefits of remote working that you can work the way you want, and not be under constant supervision of others?

Working at your own pace is really an advantage of remote work. But after having tried Remote Mob Programming for several weeks and getting a glimpse at its advantages, we are okay to give that up.

How has Remote Mob Programming changed your development flow?

It changed a lot. We no longer wait for code reviews or the merging of pull requests. Code review simply happens on the way. We no longer get distracted so easily. The mob makes sure that we stay focused and keep a constant flow.

How did you end up using Remote Mob Programming?

In August 2018, the three of us started a new project. Until then, we haven't worked together yet. We started with a kick-off week at the customer. For us, it was essential to discuss and make all fundamental decisions like service boundaries, technologies, naming, coding styles, and first and foremost, and spaces vs. tabs together. For that, we wanted to build our very first service collaboratively, and Simon had the idea to use Mob Programming. This felt so good that we continued to use Mob Programming back in home office. Until now.

Is Mob Programming simply a fit for your current task or a fit for any task?

We believe that Mob Programming is suitable for any complex task. It, however, is paramount that the team size is right (read: not too big). From our experience, we recommend a team size of four. In addition, we form a cross-functional team of an independent domain at our customer, meaning we implement clear and specific business functionality and run the software as self-contained systems.

Looking back at one year of Remote Mob Programming: What are its key advantages for you?

We learned more than ever before. But even more important, we have more time with our families than ever before.

How did your customer reacted to the fact that you're coding everything together?

Our customer invests heavily in self-organizing teams. They trust us that we do all things necessary to make the project a success. They, of course, raised questions and had comments on our way of working. But we actively communicated our progress. And it helps to deliver.

Do you feel a sense of peer pressure always sitting in front of your screen at the same time? What about breaks?

Somewhat yes. And sometimes it's annoying, because there is peer pressure. On the other way, this leads to discipline and focus, keeping Twitter and co at bay. Because of this, breaks are essential, especially for feeding the social media dragon. And, to our regret, we neglected making sufficient breaks at the beginning because of the flow. But over time, it evened out and we take a break every two hours.

How do you synchronise your working hours?

We agreed to start at 9am and have lunch at the same time each day. Clearly, one looses flexibility in their individual working hours – typically one of the key advantages of remote work. But we accept that for mob programming. And because we are a team of five people today, it's not a big issue if someone is absent because the mob still moves forward.

Do you work in the mob all the time?

Yes.

What about non-coding tasks in your mob?

We deliberately decide what's in our core domain. These analyses and meetings we do together. In every meeting, we try to work on a concrete artifact, e.g., a wiki page, a specification or a diagram. During that time, we don't change the typist role but still use screensharing.

Is your product owner part of your mob?

Our product owner also works remotely. She joins the mob on demand and when we're doing business analysis. This works quite well.

Is it really efficient when everybody works at the same issue at the same time?

Definitely yes, if you want to optimize for time to market and knowledge.

The thought of on always-on camera makes me feel a bit uncomfortable. Do you get used to it? Is it even necessary?

At first, we felt uncomfortable as well. But yes, you get used to it. And it is necessary because it significantly improves communication. It really does.

My team would like to try out Remote Mob Programming. How should we start?

That's great. We recommend to select a medium-sized feature and try it out with your standard laptop camera and microphone. One member should read the book Code with the Wisdom of the Crowd by Mark Pearl[1] to be able to act as a moderator if necessary. Regarding everything else, discover what is working for you.

---

[1] https://pragprog.com/book/mpmob

About the Authors

Jochen Christ

🐦 jochen_christ

Jochen is a senior consultant at INNOQ. As a specialist for Java technologies, he creates elegant solutions with innovative architecture concepts, such as Microservices. Jochen is interested in agile methods, clean code and usable security. He speaks at conferences and enjoys local meetups.

Simon Harrer

🐦 simonharrer

Simon is a senior consultant at INNOQ. He fights everyday for simple solutions with domain-driven design, fitting architectures such as microservices, and clean code. He wrote the book Java by Comparison[1] that helps beginners to write cleaner code through before/after comparisons.

Martin Huber

🐦 Waterback

Martin is a senior consultant at INNOQ. More than a decade of his work life is filled with the creation of integration applications in Java. He focuses on web technologies for integration challenges. In his free time, he ponders around with Python and plays and coaches American football.

Design by Sonja Scheungrab 🐦 multebaerr.

---

[1] https://java.by-comparison.com

Resources

Books

- Code with the Wisdom of the Crowd by Mark Pearl[1]
- Mob Programming by Woody Zuill and Kevin Meadows[2]
- Mob Programming Guidebook by Maaret Pyhäjärvi[3]
- Debugging Teams by Brian Fitzpatrick and Ben Collins-Sussman[4]

Videos

- Mob Programming: A Whole Team Approach by Woody Zuill[5]
- Leaping back into the code via Remote Mobbing by Sal Freudenberg[6]

Podcasts

- Episode 'Mob' in Agile in 3 Minutes by Amitai Schleier[7]
- Episode '61 Remote Mob Programming - Home but not alone' in INNOQ Podcast (German)[8]

---

[1] https://pragprog.com/book/mpmob

[2] https://leanpub.com/mobprogramming

[3] https://leanpub.com/mobprogrammingguidebook

[4] https://shop.oreilly.com/product/0636920042372.do

[5] https://www.youtube.com/watch?v=SHOVVnRB4ho

[6] https://www.pscp.tv/w/1kvKpEEklQQGE?t=24s

[7] https://agilein3minut.es/32

[8] https://www.innoq.com/de/podcast/061-remote-mob-programming/

www.ingramcontent.com/pod-product-compliance
Lightning Source LLC
LaVergne TN
LVHW051510180726
843512LV00006B/707